Meet Jesus

A Pointing Out Book

Text by Sylvia Mandeville
and Lance Pierson

Illustrations by Richard Deverell

Scripture Union

47 Marylebone Lane, London W1M 6AX

First published 1977 by
Scripture Union
47 Marylebone Lane,
London W1M 6AX

ISBN 0 85421 522 0

Designed by Tony Cantale
Research by Christine Deverell
Printed in Great Britain by
Purnell & Sons Ltd., Paulton, Bristol

Exploring the Bible

To boys and girls:

Here is a book for you, with
- stories to read
- pictures to look at
- things to do.

The book tells you a lot about Jesus and about what it was like when he was alive.

On the 'things to do' pages you will find puzzles, questions, and ideas for making things, as well as suggestions for writing and drawing.

If you get a scrap book you can stick your stories and pictures into it, and so make your own 'Meet Jesus' book.

To parents and teachers:

Boys and girls, together with parents, friends and teachers, will gain immense pleasure from exploring the five stories which comprise this book.

The Pointing Out series is, however, designed to provide not only pleasure; it is a teaching aid— for home and church. All the books are based on a threefold principle: listen, look and do—each activity complementing the others.

Our aim is not only to bring home through the use of vivid detail the content and teaching of the Bible stories, but also to help boys and girls to see and absorb the background against which the events took place. That is why in this book we have chosen to depict the stories through the eyes of an observer with whom the children can experience the events which the artist has portrayed.

As well as listening to the stories, girls and boys will love to study the two-page picture spreads, discovering a host of detail which adds interest and depth to the incidents depicted.

Both the stories and the pictures are reinforced by the material on the activity pages which sends the reader back to the pictures again and again.

As the children are involved in these activities the message of God's Word will come across in terms which are relevant to their age and experience.

Titles in this series:
Meet Jesus
God's friends

What's happening in the stable?

I must tell you what's been happening over the road. This afternoon Mother sent me up on the roof to collect some figs she had been drying. When I was there I stopped to look over into the street. It was very noisy and crowded with people. The Romans want to count all the people in the country, so they have told everybody to go back to the towns where they were born. For days now people have been arriving here in Bethlehem, and the landlord of the inn keeps turning people away. 'No room! No room! Try somewhere else!' he has been shouting.

As I was watching, I saw a tired lady ride up on a donkey led by a man. They stopped at the inn. The landlord was just going to send them away when his wife came. She stared at the two people and whispered to her husband. He nodded and went away, and his wife led them into the stable below the inn.

Suddenly she rushed back into the inn, calling to her servants to bring water. One maid ran out with a bundle of clean straw.
I didn't see what happened next because I heard my mother calling, 'Ruth, Ruth, what's keeping you?' So I had to go down. I should be helping now, but I've just come to have a quick look at the stable.

The man and his wife are still there. And I think I can hear a baby crying. But it can't be a baby, can it? Not in a dirty, smelly stable? Yes, it is. There *is* a baby. I can see it by the torch light. The landlady is wrapping it round and round with strips of cloth, and now she is giving the baby to the lady—who is looking up at the man and smiling. They both seem very happy. The baby has stopped crying now, and she is putting it very carefully on the straw in the manger.

Isn't it exciting? I must tell Mother. A baby born in the stable! I hope we can go and see him tomorrow, and perhaps we can take a present.

(You can read about Jesus being born in the stable in Luke chapter 2, verses 1 to 16.)

Some things to do . . .

Ruth

Ruth was excited because so much was happening in Bethlehem where she lived. Turn to the big picture and look at all the people. Find this rich man on his horse.

Can you also find:
- a beggar
- a Roman soldier
- a crippled man
- people sleeping

Pretend you are Ruth. Write a story about what you can see and hear, or tell someone your story.

In the stable

Find out about the people in the stable by reading Luke chapter 2, verses 1 to 7.
- What is the name of the lady? (verse 5)
- What is the name of the man? (verse 4)
- From where have they come? (verse 4)
- Why have they come to Bethlehem? (verses 3 and 4)
- Why are they in the stable? (verse 7)
- What happened after they came to the stable? (verse 7)

Jesus

Mary's baby is Jesus.
Here is a code:

1	2	3	4	5	6	7	8	9	10	11	12	13
a	b	c	d	e	f	g	h	i	j	k	l	m

14	15	16	17	18	19	20	21	22	23
n	o	p	q	r	s	t	u	v	w

24	25	26
x	y	z

Copy these coded messages about Jesus on to a sheet of paper, and work them out. The first one has been started for you.

25 15 21   23 9 12 12   14 1 13 5
y o u   w i l l
9 9 13 10 5 19 21 19
                  (Luke chapter 1, verse 31)

8 5   23 9 12 12 2 5
7 18 5 1 20
              (Luke chapter 1, verse 32)

8 5   23 9 12 12 2 5
3 1 12 12 5 4 20 8 5
19 15 14 15 6 20 8 5
13 15 19 20 8 9 7 8 7 15 4
             (Luke chapter 1, verse 32)

God sent his messenger, the angel Gabriel, to give these messages to Mary before Jesus was born. Jesus was born on the first Christmas Day.

Giving and receiving

In this picture the lady is giving money to the beggar.
At Christmas we give and receive presents.
Think of a present which you have received. Draw a picture of your present and the person who gave it to you.
Giving presents is one way of showing people that we love them. We do not have to wait for Christmas to do this.
Make a present for someone you love. Here is one idea:

A paper weight

1. Choose a smooth, clean pebble.
2. Paint a picture or pattern on it.
3. When the paint has dried, varnish the stone with clear varnish.

On the first Christmas Day God showed his love for us by giving Jesus.

The shepherds

Look at the picture of Bethlehem again. Point to the shepherds at work on the hill.
On the first Christmas Day, while it was still dark, God sent a message to the shepherds outside Bethlehem. Look in Luke chapter 2, verses 11 and 12 to see what the message was. The shepherds hurried to Bethlehem to see Jesus. They knew that Jesus was God's Son and that God loves us so much that he gave Jesus to the world. The shepherds were so happy that they told everyone they met about Jesus.
Draw a picture of them doing this.

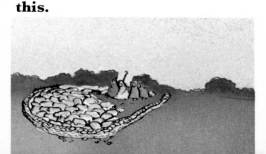

On the beach

I'd just got back to the farm after morning school when the lads from down the road raced past.

'Quick Simeon! There's something going on at the beach!'

Mum said I could go, as long as I was back in time to take Dad some lunch at midday. He was sowing corn, and it's hungry work. So I chased down the track towards Capernaum and the lake. I passed crowds of people, all going the same way.

'What's happening?' I asked.

'It's the Nazareth preacher. He's healing lots of people down on the beach.'

We had heard Jesus speak in the synagogue and he was really good. He could make people better even if they were nearly dying.

I took a short cut through the back streets of Capernaum and rushed down to the beach to find out what Jesus was doing. Nearer the lake I heard yelling and howling and I was just going to push through the crowd when someone shouted my name. The voice came from up in the sky. I looked up and saw a friend of mine perched on the branch of a tree. 'Simeon, come up here, there's a terrific view,' he called. So I climbed up after him, and crawled along the branch over the heads of the people.

Now I could see Jesus, sitting in a boat near the shore. Suddenly he started talking. I could hear him, clear as a cock-crow. He told some stories, and everyone listened, and laughed at the funny bits.

All at once he stopped, and pointed to the hillside behind the crowd. I could see Dad there, scattering his corn-seed in the field.

'Listen to this,' Jesus said. 'It's important. Look behind you.' All the heads turned round and watched Dad at work! And Jesus began talking about him.

'There goes the farmer, sowing his grain. Some seed falls on the path, and the birds gobble it up, some falls on the stony ground . . .'

But then I saw Mum. She didn't look very pleased. It was long past Dad's lunchtime. I scrambled down the tree and ran for my life.

I never heard what Jesus said next.

(You can read about Jesus teaching from the boat in Mark chapter 3, verses 7 to 10, and Mark chapter 4, verses 1 to 9.)

On the beach

Some things to do . . .

Simeon

Simeon was glad because he could see and hear Jesus. Pretend that you are Simeon. What can you see from your branch in the tree? What can you hear? Write a story about what you can see and hear or record your story on a tape recorder.

Look in Mark chapter 4, verse 1, to see why Jesus is in the boat. What is the name of the Lake? What is Jesus doing in the boat?

Some people are ill

Look at the people in the crowd. Point to the people who are ill. Jesus loved all the people, but these ill people needed his love and help in special ways.

How did Jesus show his love for these people? Matthew chapter 15, verses 29 to 31 will help you to answer this question.

The children are enjoying themselves

Find the children in the picture. Make a booklet about them. In your booklet draw pictures to show what the children are doing.

You can find out about Jesus and children from Matthew chapter 19, verses 13 to 15. The disciples tried to send the children away, but what did Jesus say? Write Jesus' words on the cover of your booklet.

Some people are working

A lot of people in the story are working hard. How many different jobs can you see? What are the jobs?

The story Jesus told

Find the story in Mark chapter 4, verses 1 to 9, and read it. Draw a series of four pictures to illustrate the story. In your pictures show the different kinds of soil on which the seeds fell.

Jesus talked about this story with some of his friends. Read Mark chapter 4, verse 20. What do we need to do if we want to be followers of Jesus?

An experiment

Do an experiment to find out what makes plants grow well. You need six jars or containers (one with a lid), mustard seed, cotton wool, and water.

Jar 1: put dry seeds on dry cotton wool.

Jar 2: put seeds on wet cotton wool. Put a lid on top of the jar.

Jar 3: put seeds on wet cotton wool. Leave in a cold, light place.

Jar 4: put seeds on wet cotton wool. Leave in a warm, light place.

Jar 5: put seeds on wet cotton wool. Leave in a warm, dark place.

Jar 6: put seeds on wet cotton wool. Leave in a cold, dark place.

Leave your experiment for several days and see what happens. Which seeds grow best?

Flags and shouting

My name is James and I want to tell you about the great procession which I joined yesterday.

It happened like this. I went up on the city wall to deliver a message to my master, who is an officer in the Roman army. He and his men have been sent to Jerusalem to keep guard during our Jewish holidays in case there's any trouble.

While I was on the wall I heard shouting and cheering in the distance. So I had a look over the top, and saw a huge crowd coming up the hilly road from the Mount of Olives. People were jumping up and down and yelling and running backwards and forwards. I couldn't think what it was all about, but I could see that the soldiers on guard were worried. They were watching closely in case there was a fight. And two of our Jewish leaders came up on the wall and stood muttering together.

When I looked back at the crowd, I suddenly saw him—a man on a donkey in the middle of all the people. Some of the men and children had started climbing trees, breaking down branches, and waving them at him like flags. Other people were spreading their cloaks on the ground for the donkey to tread on. And all the time everyone was shouting.

The crowd came nearer, and then I recognized the man. It was Jesus! I knew about Jesus. My master's friend in Capernaum had a slave who had been ill, and Jesus had made him better. All the servants have been talking about him.

Soon all I could hear was the cheering crowd, calling out:
 'God bless the king who comes in the name of the Lord. Peace in heaven and glory to God.'
When the two important Jews on the wall heard these words they frowned and shook their fists at Jesus. It looked more as if they would like to kill him than welcome him as king. But I didn't bother about them. I ran down to get a branch for myself because I wanted to wave a flag as Jesus rode by. Just as he reached the gates I joined in the cry: 'God bless the king. God bless the king.'

(You can read about Jesus riding into Jerusalem in Luke chapter 19, verses 28 to 40.)

Some things to do . . .

The Roman army

James took a message to a centurion in the Roman army. Look at the large picture and point to the Roman soldiers. Where are they, and what are they doing?
The Romans had captured Jerusalem and the land of Palestine where the Jewish people lived. Find out all you can about the Roman army. Use some books from school or the library to help you. Draw a large picture of a centurion. Make sure his uniform is accurate and paste foil or silver paper on to his metal armour.
Write a story about your centurion.

The procession

From the city wall James could see a Jewish procession. Everybody was cheering Jesus.
You can read about this procession in the Bible. Find Luke chapter 19, verses 28 to 38.

Jesus the king

Unjumble the words to find the answers to the questions below.
1. **Where was Jesus going?** (verse 28)
   He going to was Jerusalem
2. **What did Jesus tell two disciples to do?** (verse 30)
   village Go the to and get colt a
   Find the village in the picture.
3. **What was special about the colt?** (verse 30)
   never It been ridden had
4. **What did the two disciples say when they were asked why they took the colt?** (verse 34)
   needs Master The it
5. **What did the people do as Jesus rode the colt?** (verse 36)
   They cloaks spread their road on the
6. **What did the people shout as Jesus rode the colt?** (verse 38)
   God the king bless who comes the Lord in the name of

Look at the large picture and find this boy in the tree. Pretend you have climbed the tree with him. You are cheering Jesus because he loves everyone and teaches them about God. He is the king.
Write a story about being in the crowd on the day Jesus rode into Jerusalem. You could draw some pictures to illustrate your story.

Look at Jesus

Make a model

The trees
16cm — 16cm — 6cm
1. Colour green and brown both sides.
2. Cut along lines.
3. Roll up.
4. Paste edges of brown section.

The people
12cm
1. Cut circles into quarters.
2. Draw face and clothes.
3. Make into cone and paste.
4. Cut out arms. Colour sleeves. Paste on figure.

God bless the King

Assemble your model on a tray or polystyrene tile and make a flag to stand by your model. On the flag write: **'God bless the king.'**
Make two or three more figures but give them *angry faces*.
Read Luke chapter 19, verse 39 and find out what these angry men were called. Here are the letters which make up their name:
R E E S S H I A P

On trial for his life

I've just had the saddest day of my life. It started very early this morning when it was still dark. I was woken up suddenly by the sound of crying. It was my mistress, who is the wife of Pilate, the Roman Governor of Jerusalem.

'Julia!' she shouted to me. 'Where is my husband? I must speak to Pilate. I've had a terrible dream.'

I ran to her, and helped her to get dressed. Pilate was not in his room, so we went to look for him. Outside the great Judgement Hall we found soldiers on guard who said that there was an important trial going on. We both crept into the Hall and then my mistress grabbed my arm. 'That's him. That's the man I dreamt about,' she said, pointing to the prisoner. It was Jesus.

My mistress hurried to a guard. 'You must take a message to my husband,' she said. 'Tell him that that man has done nothing wrong. I have had an awful dream about him.'

Although the guard went to Pilate with the message, Pilate took no notice. He walked slowly out of the Judgement Hall to the courtyard outside, with Jesus following him. It was very quiet. Suddenly I had a shock. Outside the entrance I saw some of the Jewish leaders, and behind them a crowd of rough-looking men, all waiting for Pilate. He asked them what they wanted him to do with Jesus, and they started yelling out, 'Kill him! Crucify him!' I felt sick, and my mistress turned pale, and started to cry. 'Tell me what happens, I can't watch any more,' she said, and left me standing by the pillar.

I could see that the crowd hated Jesus, and didn't want Pilate to set him free. Pilate knew this too. At last he called for a bowl of water, and he washed his hands in front of all those people. 'This is to show you that it's not my fault if Jesus dies. It's what you want,' he said.

'We don't care. We'll take the blame,' they all screamed back, while Jesus stood very still and said nothing at all.

Soon after that the soldiers took him away. At nine o'clock this morning they nailed him to a cross outside the city walls.

(You can read about Jesus and Pilate in Matthew chapter 27, verses 11 to 26.)

Some things to do . . .

Julia

Find Julia in the big picture. She is standing with her back to you and is looking at Pilate and Jesus.
Here are some Romans who are also watching Pilate. They are all wearing white togas.

Point to these other people:
- Roman soldiers
- Jesus
- Pilate
- A servant
- Pilate's wife
- Jewish leaders, who would not come inside the Roman building.

■ Pretend that you are Julia and that you are writing to your family. In your letter describe some of the people you can see and say what they are doing.

Pontius Pilate

Pontius Pilate was the Roman Governor who was in charge of Jerusalem.
Use some books from the library to find out what a Roman Governor did.
Find Pilate's chariot. Draw pictures of the kinds of transport a Governor, Prime Minister or Queen may use today.

Pilate's wife

What did Pilate's wife say about Jesus? Sort out these words to find the answer:
WITH THAT HAVE NOTHING INNOCENT TO DO MAN
(Matthew chapter 27, verse 19)

The trial

Julia said that there was a trial taking place. What happens at a trial? If the judge finds that someone has done wrong he decides what the punishment should be.
People who do wrong deserve to be punished.
Here are some things which Jesus did:
- Healed the sick people
- Taught about God
- Fed the hungry

What did Jesus do that was wrong? Sort out these letters to find the answer: T H N O G N I
Jesus did not deserve to be punished.
What did Pilate say about Jesus?

Sort out these words to find the answer:
I HIM GUILTY HAVE FOUND NOT
(Luke chapter 23, verse 14)

The crowd

What did the crowd shout about Jesus? Sort out these words to find the answer:
HIM CRUCIFY
(Matthew chapter 27, verse 23)

Draw the crowd. Above the crowd draw some speech balloons and in them write what the people said. Copy these words underneath your picture: '*The people said, "We have a law that says he ought to die, because he claimed to be the Son of God."*'
(John chapter 19, verse 7)

The Son of God

Jesus is the Son of God.
Three days after he died he rose from the dead, and now he is alive. Only the Son of God could do this. It is hard to understand why Jesus had to die. This is what the Bible says:
'God made us his friends through the death of his Son.'
● Draw a poster with these words on it from Romans chapter 5, verse 10. Design your poster, and colour or paint it. Write the letters in pencil before you colour them.

Good news

Ben, our donkey, ran away during the night, and as soon as it was light Dad sent me to find him. I was hunting through the back streets of Jerusalem thinking how quiet and fresh everything was, when I heard running footsteps. Then my mother's friend, Mary, and some other women rushed past me and knocked at a door.

A man came. 'We've got to talk to you,' they said. 'They've taken Jesus' body out of the tomb, and we don't know where they've put him.'

The women went into the house, and immediately afterwards two men dashed out, flinging on their cloaks, and ran down towards the city gates. The men were Peter and John who had been two of Jesus' best friends. Then Mary came out again, and went after them slowly, crying.

I wanted to follow Mary, but I had to find Ben. So I went on searching and thinking about what I had heard, until I came to the edge of the city.

Outside on the hill I could see the cross where Jesus had died two days before. Jesus had been good to everybody—and yet they had killed him. Now even his body had gone from the tomb. I couldn't understand.

Suddenly I heard someone calling my name. 'Jacob, have you heard the news about Jesus?' It was my cousin, Rachel. 'I've just met Mary and she told me.'

'I've seen Mary, too,' I said. 'She was crying.'

'She's not crying now,' said Rachel. 'It's wonderful news. This morning she went down to Jesus' tomb twice. The second time she was standing by herself, outside the cave. It was empty and she thought the body had been stolen.'

'I know,' I said.

'Then suddenly she saw a man. She thought he was the gardener, and she asked him if he had moved the body from the cave. But it wasn't the gardener. It was Jesus himself! He spoke to Mary and told her to come back here with the news. He says he will be meeting us all again, soon.'

Rachel was so excited that she hugged me. And I was so excited that I didn't mind. Ben had to wait. I rushed home to tell everyone that Jesus is alive.

(You can read about what happened when Mary went to the tomb in John chapter 20, verses 1 to 18.)

Some things to do . . .

Good news

Find Ben in the garden. While Jacob was hunting for his donkey he heard some good news. What was it? Write a list, or draw pictures of some good news which you have heard this week.

Being alive

Here are some things which you can do because you are alive:

- eating
- playing with friends
- watching television

Think of some more things you can do. Draw pictures of the things you enjoy doing.

Remember you can only do these things because you are alive.

The crosses

When Jacob was looking for Ben he saw these crosses. They reminded him that Jesus had died and that Jesus' body had been put in a grave or tomb outside the city.

Jacob saw two men running towards the city gate which led to this tomb. You can read about the men in John chapter 20, verses 1 to 10.

What day was it? (verse 1)
Where were they going? (verse 3)
What did they find in the tomb? (verses 6 and 7)

Mary Magdalene

Peter and John ran away from the tomb. Look in John chapter 20, verse 10 to find out where they were going. Mary stayed in the garden. She was sad because she did not know where Jesus' body was. Whom did she meet in the garden? You can find this part of the story in John chapter 20, verses 11 to 18. Draw a picture of Mary after she knew that Jesus is alive.

The empty tomb

Here is something which Jesus said to his disciples *before* he rode the colt into Jerusalem:

' I must go to Jerusalem and suffer . . . I will be put to death but three days later I will be raised to life' (Matthew chapter 16, verse 21).

Look at the big picture:

- find the city
- find the crosses

- find the tomb
- find Jesus

Now sort out these jumbled words. They tell you about the things you have just been looking at:

- The city is JREUSLAEM where Jesus SFFUREDE.
- The cross is where Jesus DDIE.
- The tomb is ETMPY.
- Jesus is LIVAE.

Everything happened as Jesus said it would.

The garden

Look at these flowers, and then find them in the big picture. They all grow near Jerusalem.

From left to right the flowers are: cyclamen, almond, tulip and narcissus.

Make your own small garden in an old dish or on a tray. Use small plants, twigs, moss, soil and stones. Make an empty tomb in your garden to remind you that Jesus is alive.

Jesus is alive

Jacob was thrilled when he heard that Jesus is alive. Pretend that you are Jacob telling your family the good news which you have heard. Write down what you would say. Do not forget to make your news sound exciting.

When we hear good news we often dance or sing. Make up a dance of your own or sing a song which you know about Jesus being alive.

- Write a thank you prayer about Jesus being alive.